THE BEST
TENNIS
PLAYERS
OF ALL TIME

By Marty Gitlin

www.abdopublishing.com

Published by Abdo Publishing, a division of ABDO, PO Box 398166, Minneapolis, Minnesota 55439. Copyright © 2015 by Abdo Consulting Group, Inc. International copyrights reserved in all countries. No part of this book may be reproduced in any form without written permission from the publisher. SportsZone™ is a trademark and logo of Abdo Publishing.

Printed in the United States of America, North Mankato, Minnesota
092014
012015

THIS BOOK CONTAINS
RECYCLED MATERIALS

Cover Photos: PRS/AP Images, left; Michel Spingler/AP Images, right
Interior Photos: PRS/AP Images, 1 (left); Michel Spingler/AP Images, 1 (right); AP Images, 7, 13, 15, 17, 25, 29, 45; Bodini/AP Images, 9; John Rooney/AP Images, 11; Adam Stoltman/AP Images, 19, 27; MAC/AP Images, 21; Marty Lederhandler/AP Images, 23; Laurent Rebours/AP Images, 31; Richard Drew/AP Images, 33; Burnett/AP Images, 35; Bob Dear/AP Images, 37; Lance Jeffrey/AP Images, 39; Dave Caulkin/AP Images, 41, 49; Michel Euler/AP Images, 43; Mark Lennihan/AP Images, 47; Neale Cousland/Shutterstock Images, 51, 55; Anthony Correia/Shutterstock Images, 53; Lev Radin/Shutterstock Images, 57; Alessia Pierdomenico/AP Images, 59; Olga Besnard/AP Images, 61

Editor: Patrick Donnelly
Series Designer: Christa Schneider

Library of Congress Control Number: 2014944205

Cataloging-in-Publication Data
Gitlin, Marty.
 The best tennis players of all time / Marty Gitlin.
   p. cm. -- (Sports' best ever)
ISBN 978-1-62403-622-4 (lib. bdg.)
Includes bibliographical references and index.
1. Tennis--Juvenile literature.   I. Title.
796.342--dc23
                                        2014944205

TABLE OF CONTENTS

INTRODUCTION

The world's best tennis players are wizards with rackets. Yet their grit and guts might be even more impressive.

Tennis is an unforgiving game. Matches are long. The weather can be extreme. And on the court, all eyes are focused on just two or four players. It takes amazing agility, power, stamina, and mental strength to excel in tennis. Those who do become stars. And those who can win in the Grand Slams—the Australian Open, the French Open, the US Open, and Wimbledon—become legends.

Here are some of the greatest tennis players of all time.

ROD LAVER

The date was September 10, 1962. The place was Forest Hills, New York. The event was the men's final at the US Championships, the precursor to the US Open.

The two best tennis players in the world were showing off their talents. But Rod Laver was making better shots than fellow Australian Roy Emerson. Emerson was the defending champion. But he had no chance. Laver hit the ball so hard that Emerson barely had time to react. The left-hander broke Emerson's serve to open the fourth set and cruised to victory. When it was over, Laver tossed his racket in the air and smiled. It might have been his first smile since the tournament had begun.

Rod Laver raised the Wimbledon trophy four times in his stellar career.

It was not just any victory. With it, "The Rocket" became the first player since 1938 to have won all four Grand Slam events in a single year. Nobody knows how many others Laver could have won. He turned professional in 1963. That made him ineligible to play in Grand Slam events. But he was ready when the Open Era began in 1968. Grand Slam events became open to professional players that year. And in 1969, he became the first player to win all four Grand Slam events in the same year twice.

Laver is regarded as the best player of his era. His 200 career tournament titles rank number one in tennis history through 2014. Laver also won 11 Grand Slam singles crowns, despite not being allowed to play in them from 1963 to 1967. And he even won five Davis Cups, which is the top international team tournament in men's tennis.

2

The number of men with at least two championships in each of the four Grand Slam tournaments—Rod Laver and Roy Emerson.

Rod Laver is the only man to win the Grand Slam twice, as of 2014.

ROD LAVER

Hometown: Rockhampton, Queensland, Australia

Height, Weight: 5 feet 8, 150 pounds

Birth Date: August 9, 1938

Tournament Titles: 200

Grand Slam Singles Titles: 11
Australian Open: 3 (1960, 1962, 1969)
French Open: 2 (1962, 1969)
Wimbledon: 4 (1961, 1962, 1968, 1969)
US Open: 2 (1962, 1969)

Davis Cup Titles: 5 (1959–62, 1973)

MARGARET
COURT

It had been 17 years since a woman had won the Grand Slam. But Margaret Court was just one point away from achieving that feat. It was September 12, 1970. Court faced match point in the US Open final against Rosie Casals.

A deep shot forced Court to retreat. But she was a powerful hitter. The Australian leaned back and smashed a powerful forehand. Casals missed the return. Court had captured the coveted Grand Slam.

She did not toss her racket into the air. She did not even raise her arms in triumph. She merely jogged to the net to shake hands. She was just glad the pressure was off.

"When you win the Grand Slam . . . you sort of thank God it is over and then you wonder if you can really play with that motivation anymore," Court said.

Margaret Court celebrates her title at the 1973 US Open, her final Grand Slam singles victory.

Court did, however, play with enough motivation to thrive into her thirties. And she nearly swept the four Grand Slam events again in 1973. That year she won the Australian, French, and US Opens. She still held the women's record with 24 Grand Slam victories through 2014. Her 11 Australian Open triumphs also remained the most ever by one player in a single Grand Slam event.

Court used an attacking serve-and-volley style that overpowered opponents. She was also mobile for her size. That allowed her to cover the entire court. Many consider her the greatest women's tennis player of all time.

40

The number of combined Grand Slam doubles and mixed doubles titles Margaret Court earned, a record at the time of her retirement in 1977.

Mobile and athletic, Margaret Court covered a lot of ground on the tennis court.

MARGARET COURT

Hometown: Perth, Australia

Height, Weight: 5 feet 9, 149 pounds

Birth Date: July 16, 1942

Tournament Titles: 192

Grand Slam Singles Titles: 24
    Australian Open: 11 (1960–66, 1969–71, 1973)
    French Open: 5 (1962, 1964, 1969, 1970, 1973)
    Wimbledon: 3 (1963, 1965, 1970)
    US Open: 5 (1962, 1965, 1969, 1970, 1973)

BILLIE JEAN KING

The most memorable match in the brilliant career of Billie Jean King was not a Grand Slam final. It was not even a match against another woman. It came in what was known as the "Battle of the Sexes."

The match was played on September 20, 1973. More than 30,000 fans packed the Houston Astrodome. Another 90 million television viewers tuned in. They watched King play former men's champion Bobby Riggs. Riggs claimed he could beat any female player. And King accepted the challenge.

King knew she had to win for women everywhere. "I thought it would set us back 50 years if I didn't win that match," she said. "It would ruin the women's tour and affect all women's self-esteem."

Billie Jean King shows off the winner's trophy after she defeated Bobby Riggs in the "Battle of the Sexes."

King did more than just win. She dominated Riggs. But then, King was used to dominating on the tennis court. She had emerged as an elite player after winning her first Wimbledon title in 1966. In 1972 she became just the fifth woman to win every Grand Slam singles title.

King played an aggressive style. She used her quickness and speed to rush the net and finish off points. Her intensity and concentration allowed her to beat the best players in the world in pressure situations. Even as her playing career wound down, King remained an important figure in tennis and the sports world. She founded the Women's Tennis Association, the governing body of the women's tour. She also founded the Women's Sports Foundation to help shine a light on issues in women's sports. Just like on that night in Houston, King continued taking stands to help all women.

20

The number of combined Wimbledon singles, doubles, and mixed doubles titles Billie Jean King earned. She shared the record with Martina Navratilova through 2014.

Billie Jean King was known for her aggressive style of play.

BILLIE JEAN KING

Hometown: Long Beach, California

Height, Weight: 5 feet 4, 134 pounds

Birth Date: November 22, 1943

Tournament Titles: 129

Grand Slam Singles Titles: 12
Australian Open: 1 (1968)
French Open: 1 (1972)
Wimbledon: 6 (1966–68, 1972, 1973, 1975)
US Open: 4 (1967, 1971, 1972, 1974)

JIMMY CONNORS

Jimmy Connors was close to winning his second US Open. The floppy-haired American held a 5–4 lead in the fourth set against Bjorn Borg in the 1976 finals. But he had blown two match points.

Connors then unleashed his famous two-handed backhand. He slammed one deep into the court and rushed the net. Borg tried to lob it over Connors's head but sent it out of bounds. Connors had his third match point. A serve and volley forced another Borg error. Connors flipped his racket into the air and raised his arms in triumph. He had yet another championship.

Jimmy Connors demonstrates his patented two-handed backhand.

The tennis world was getting used to it. Connors was a major figure in the growing popularity of tennis in the 1970s. He won three Grand Slam titles in 1974 alone. And his brash personality created as much interest in the sport as his brilliant play. Tennis fans either loved or hated him.

401

The number of tournaments Jimmy Connors played in during his career.

Connors boasted a unique style. He hit flat shots with no topspin. But he could still slam forehands and backhands inches above the net and deep into the court. He thrived both at the baseline and at the net. And he won on all surfaces. He is the only player in history to win the US Open on grass, clay, and hard court. His game had no weaknesses.

Unlike others who retired early, Connors kept playing and winning. He won eight Grand Slam events from 1974 to 1983, during the peak era of tennis competition. Connors even won a match at the US Open at the age of 40.

Jimmy Connors enjoyed entertaining the crowd, both with his game and his on-court antics.

JIMMY CONNORS

Hometown: Santa Barbara, California

Height, Weight: 5 feet 10, 155 pounds

Birth Date: September 2, 1952

Tournament Titles: 109

Grand Slam Singles Titles: 8
    Australian Open: 1 (1974)
    Wimbledon: 2 (1974, 1982)
    US Open: 5 (1974, 1976, 1978, 1982, 1983)

Davis Cup Title: 1 (1981)

CHRIS EVERT

At the 1971 US Open, Chris Evert was a 16-year-old giant killer. The ponytailed teenager was the talk of tennis. Fans talked about her poise under pressure. They talked about her deadly baseline strokes. And they talked about her incredible run of victories.

Evert cruised through her first four matches, beating older, more experienced players. She reached the semifinals before falling to Billie Jean King, the greatest player in the world. Some players resented the publicity given to Evert. But King was not one of them.

"Chris has really helped women's tennis," King said after their match. "What it needs is more personalities."

At age 16, Chris Evert made a surprise run to the US Open semifinals.

Evert had a long run at the top of the sport. She won 18 Grand Slams from 1974 to 1986. Her seven French Open and six US Open titles were both records through 2013. She also became the first woman in 40 years to win four straight US Opens. And she finished the year ranked as the world's top singles player seven times from 1974 to 1981.

Evert was a baseline master. She picked apart opponents with her deadly forehand and two-handed backhand. She could angle shots better than anyone. And she never let anger or frustration get the best of her. That calmness helped her become one of the greatest players of her generation.

13

The number of consecutive years in which Chris Evert won at least one Grand Slam title, a record through 2013.

Chris Evert fires her two-hand backhand from behind the baseline in 1975.

CHRIS EVERT

Hometown: Boca Raton, Florida

Height, Weight: 5 feet 6, 126 pounds

Birth Date: December 21, 1954

Tournament Titles: 157

Grand Slam Singles Titles: 18
Australian Open: 2 (1982, 1984)
French Open: 7 (1974, 1975, 1979, 1980, 1983, 1985, 1986)
Wimbledon: 3 (1974, 1976, 1981)
US Open: 6 (1975–78, 1980, 1982)

BJORN BORG

The 1980 Wimbledon men's final was nearing four hours. On one side of the court stood stoic Swedish superstar Bjorn Borg. On the other side was brash young American John McEnroe.

The British crowd delighted in an epic fourth-set tiebreaker. McEnroe had survived to send the match into a fifth set. Borg finally earned match point. McEnroe served and raced to the net. Borg whipped his trademark two-handed backhand past him. Game, set, match. Borg had won his fifth straight Wimbledon championship.

The Swede with the flowing blond hair was known for his dominance at Wimbledon. But he also won six French Open titles. His 141–16 record in Grand Slam events remained the best in men's tennis history through 2014.

Bjorn Borg celebrates after beating John McEnroe for his fifth Wimbledon title.

Borg rarely showed emotion on the court. But English novelist Tim Pears believed Borg learned to not display his passion for the sport. "His heart was filled with joy for this game and . . . he hid this joy not to deny it, but rather to nurture its presence within him."

Borg was a wizard with a racket in his hand. He sprayed shots wherever he wanted. His topspin forehand and backhand jumped when they hit the court. And he was the best at blasting the ball past opponents who dared rush the net.

Borg played in one of the strongest eras in men's tennis. Yet he was ranked number one in the world for a total of 109 weeks between 1977 and 1981.

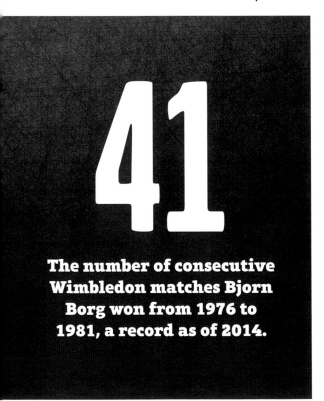

41

The number of consecutive Wimbledon matches Bjorn Borg won from 1976 to 1981, a record as of 2014.

It is no wonder that he was inducted into the International Tennis Hall of Fame in 1987.

Bjorn Borg is carried off the court after he clinched Sweden's first-ever Davis Cup title in 1975.

BJORN BORG

Hometown: Stockholm, Sweden

Height, Weight: 5 feet 11, 159 pounds

Birth Date: June 6, 1956

Tournament Titles: 64

Grand Slam Singles Titles: 11
    French Open: 6 (1974, 1975, 1978–81)
    Wimbledon: 5 (1976–80)

Davis Cup Title: 1 (1975)

MARTINA NAVRATILOVA

At the 1981 Australian Open, budding superstar Martina Navratilova was on the verge of a huge victory. She had forged match point in the finals against Chris Evert, the top-ranked player in the world.

It had been an epic clash between contrasting styles. Navratilova was a left-handed, serve-and-volley player. The right-handed Evert was content to stay on the baseline and hit ground strokes. But now Navratilova could taste victory. She blasted a serve to Evert's backhand and sprinted forward. She followed with a drop volley that Evert hit into the net.

Martina Navratilova in action at the 1986 French Open

It was over. Navratilova jumped for joy and pumped her fist. Such rejoicing would become a familiar sight. Navratilova won six straight Grand Slam events in 1983 and 1984. She captured seven more before ending her career with an incredible 167 singles titles. Her career match record was 1,438–212. And she was ranked number one in the world for 331 weeks. She also dominated in doubles.

"She's the greatest singles, doubles, and mixed doubles player who's ever lived," said fellow tennis legend Billie Jean King.

Navratilova set a record in women's tennis with a 74-match winning streak. In doubles, her dominance was even more astounding. Her 41 doubles and mixed doubles titles at Grand Slam events were a record through 2013. She even won a mixed doubles title at the US Open at age 49.

177

The number of doubles titles Martina Navratilova won during her career.

Martina Navratilova hoists the winner's trophy at the 1983 US Open.

MARTINA NAVRATILOVA

Hometown: Prague, Czechoslovakia

Height, Weight: 5 feet 8, 144 pounds

Birth Date: October 18, 1956

Tournament Titles: 167

Grand Slam Singles Titles: 18
Australian Open: 3 (1981, 1983, 1985)
French Open: 2 (1982, 1984)
Wimbledon: 9 (1978, 1979, 1982–87, 1990)
US Open: 4 (1983, 1984, 1986, 1987)

JOHN McENROE

John McEnroe and Mats Wilander had been battling for more than six hours. Both players were exhausted. It was the 1982 Davis Cup quarterfinals in St. Louis, Missouri. McEnroe was representing the United States against Sweden.

McEnroe had finally earned match point in the fifth set. He blasted a service return, then a backhand. Wilander hit his next shot into the net. It was over. McEnroe had given the US team a victory in the deciding match.

McEnroe had won bigger matches in his amazing career. He had already earned four Grand Slam titles. But none had required more stamina. And after beating Wilander, he led the United States to its fourth Davis Cup title in five years.

John McEnroe was never one to hide his emotions on the court.

The feisty left-hander was ranked number one in the world from 1981 to 1984. He was known as much for his angry outbursts on the court as he was for his greatness. Fans and media members nicknamed him "Superbrat."

But McEnroe sure could play. He overpowered opponents with his aggressive serve-and-volley style. He won four US Opens and three Wimbledon championships from 1979 to 1984. He played nearly perfect tennis in the 1984 Wimbledon final with a 6–1, 6–1, 6–2 defeat of Jimmy Connors.

McEnroe will forever be remembered for yelling at line judges. He even screamed at himself for unforced errors. But his greatness as a tennis player will also never be forgotten.

148

The number of singles and doubles titles combined that John McEnroe won.

John McEnroe was an aggressive yet graceful player.

JOHN MCENROE

Hometown: New York, New York

Height, Weight: 5 feet 11, 165 pounds

Birth Date: February 16, 1959

Tournament Titles: 77

Grand Slam Singles Titles: 7
  Wimbledon: 3 (1981, 1983, 1984)
  US Open: 4 (1979–81, 1984)

Davis Cup Titles: 5 (1978, 1979, 1981, 1982, 1992)

STEFFI GRAF

It was match point at the 1988 US Open final. Gabriela Sabatini hit a topspin forehand and rushed the net. Young star Steffi Graf blasted a backhand that forced Sabatini to lunge to return. Graf then ripped another backhand that Sabatini could not handle.

Game, set, match, Grand Slam. The ponytailed German had become the first women's player in 18 years to win all four majors in a calendar year. But she did not toss her racket into the air in celebration. She did not fall to the ground. She did not even break a smile. Her lack of excitement was detailed by *Sports Illustrated* writer Curry Kirkpatrick.

"Her emotions seem to run the gamut from A to B: from apathy to boredom," he wrote. "Surely she knew what she was accomplishing. Certainly she realized her place in history."

Steffi Graf completed the Grand Slam by winning the US Open in 1988.

But Graf's stoic demeanor hid a competitive fire that helped make her an elite player among her peers. She followed that US Open championship by winning four of the next five Grand Slam events. She beat legend Martina Navratilova in the 1989 Wimbledon and US Open finals.

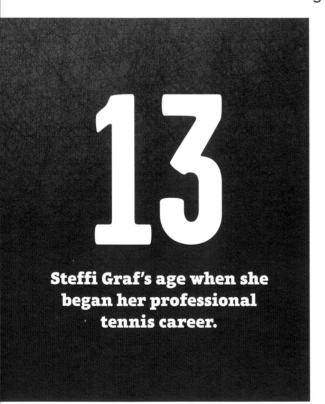

13

Steffi Graf's age when she began her professional tennis career.

Graf played a power baseline game. She directed action with hard ground strokes that kept opponents on their heels. She won four straight Grand Slam events in 1993 and 1994. And she captured six more in 1995 and 1996. Graf retired with 22 Grand Slam titles. Only Margaret Court had won more through 2014.

Graf finished the year ranked number one in the world a record eight times. In the end, it did not matter that she showed little emotion. It only mattered that she showed her greatness.

Steffi Graf shows off the form that earned her the nickname "Fraulein Forehand."

STEFFI GRAF

Hometown: Mannheim, West Germany

Height, Weight: 5 feet 9, 141 pounds

Birth Date: June 14, 1969

Tournament Titles: 107

Grand Slam Singles Titles: 22
  Australian Open: 4 (1988–90, 1994)
  French Open: 6 (1987, 1988, 1993, 1995, 1996, 1999)
  Wimbledon: 7 (1988, 1989, 1991–93, 1995, 1996)
  US Open: 5 (1988, 1989, 1993, 1995, 1996)

ANDRE AGASSI

Andre Agassi had already won a championship on the grass courts of Wimbledon. He had already captured a crown on the hard courts of the US Open and the Australian Open. But he had never bagged a title on the slow clay courts of the French Open.

Winning all four Grand Slam events is a rare feat. Each court favors a different style of play. But Agassi was on the verge of accomplishing the feat in 1999. When he smashed a serve that Andrei Medvedev returned long, it was over. The American had won the French Open. He had completed a career Grand Slam.

Agassi had not reached the French Open final in eight years. That made his victory even sweeter. He covered his face and broke into tears. "I never dreamed I'd ever be back here after so many years," he said. "I'm so proud."

Andre Agassi celebrates after clinching a career Grand Slam by winning the 1999 French Open.

Agassi began his professional career at age 16. He was one of the hottest young stars in the game. He had long hair and wore flashy clothes on the court. But he also had great skills. He won three Grand Slam titles and an Olympic gold medal through 1996. But after struggling through some personal issues off the court, it looked as though his career might be over.

Agassi returned in style, winning the French and US Opens in 1999. He was especially dominant throughout his career in the Australian Open, which he won four times.

Agassi was a baseline specialist in a time of power players. His ground strokes and service returns were among the best in the sport.

Agassi spent 52 weeks ranked number one in the world in 1999 and 2000. But his victory at the 1999 French Open was his signature moment. It proved he could win on any court at any time.

$177 million

The amount raised by the Andre Agassi Charitable Foundation through 2013.

In his younger days Andre Agassi was known as much for his flashy image as his game.

ANDRE AGASSI

Hometown: Las Vegas, Nevada

Height, Weight: 5 feet 11, 176 pounds

Birth Date: April 29, 1970

Tournament Titles: 60

Grand Slam Singles Titles: 8
　　Australian Open: 4 (1995, 2000, 2001, 2003)
　　French Open: 1 (1999)
　　Wimbledon: 1 (1992)
　　US Open: 2 (1994, 1999)

Davis Cup Titles: 3 (1990, 1992, 1995)

PETE SAMPRAS

It was September 9, 1990. Pete Sampras had just turned 19. He was supposed to be battling fellow American Andre Agassi for the US Open title. But this was really no battle. Sampras had dominated the match from the first shot of the first set.

On match point, Sampras blasted a backhand service return. Agassi hit a forehand into the net. And it was over. Sampras had barely broken a sweat in winning his first Grand Slam title. But he was too young to understand how he did it. "I didn't know what I was doing," he said years later. "I was just a new kid. Everything I did worked."

Pete Sampras became the youngest man to win the US Open when he defeated Andre Agassi in 1990.

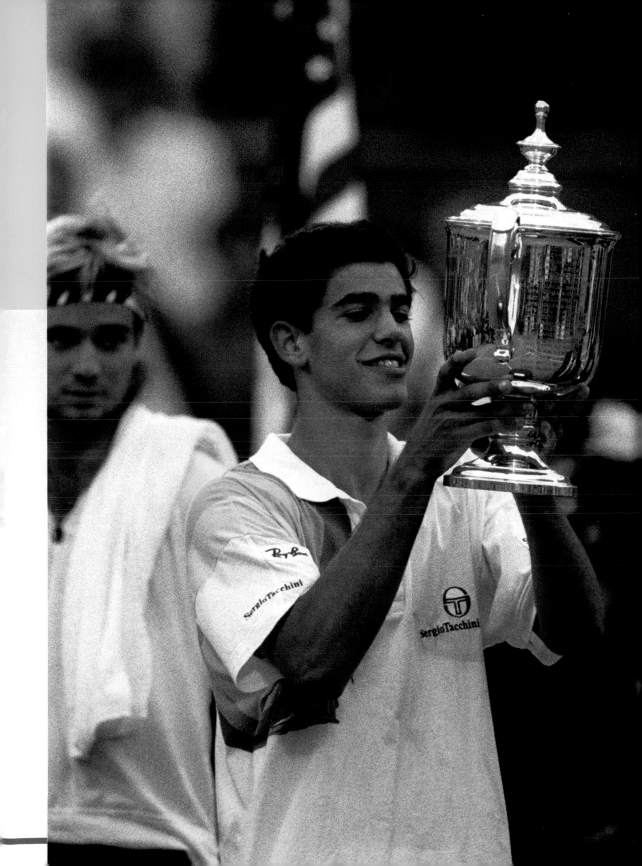

Sampras might not have known what he was doing that day, but he figured it out soon enough. He was on top of his game from his days as a fresh-faced teenager to his later years as a grizzled veteran. His silky smooth strokes and great stamina wore down opponents. He glided around the court and used a powerful serve-and-volley approach to win points quickly.

Few players matched Sampras's dominance on the grass courts of Wimbledon. Sampras won seven finals on those hallowed grounds. In fact, he never lost a Wimbledon final. But he also dominated the biggest event in his home country. Sampras won five US Open crowns from 1990 to 2002.

0

The number of service breaks in a four-set US Open quarterfinal between Pete Sampras and Andre Agassi in 2001. Sampras won the match 6–7, 7–6, 7–6, 7–6.

Sampras finished six straight seasons ranked number one in the world, a record that still stood through 2013. He captured eight Grand Slam finals without losing a set. And he went down as one of the greatest American players of all time.

Pete Sampras was especially dominant at Wimbledon, where he won seven titles.

PETE SAMPRAS

Hometown: Los Angeles, California

Height, Weight: 6 feet 1, 170 pounds

Birth Date: August 12, 1971

Tournament Titles: 64

Grand Slam Singles Titles: 14
    Australian Open: 2 (1994, 1997)
    Wimbledon: 7 (1993–95, 1997–2000)
    US Open: 5 (1990, 1993, 1995, 1996, 2002)

Davis Cup Titles: 2 (1992, 1995)

ROGER FEDERER

Roger Federer was in fine form in the 2010 Australian Open final. The tennis magician had already won the first two sets against Andy Murray. Now Federer was going for a clean sweep. But the Swiss superstar needed to win the third-set tiebreaker.

Federer blasted a forehand on an angle few players could dream of hitting. He rushed the net and sliced a backhand. The ball barely cleared the net. Murray waved at it in vain. Then Federer ripped a forehand so hard and so deep that Murray could not touch it. Soon it was over. Federer had won his sixteenth Grand Slam title and fourth Australian Open.

Federer usually played well in Australia. But he was masterful at Wimbledon. He won that tournament six times between 2003 and 2009. He then surprised his critics by winning it again in 2012.

In the prime of his career, Roger Federer was a master on every playing surface.

In his prime, Federer was the master of all. He could place the ball anywhere on the court with power. He won championships on clay courts, grass courts, and hard courts. He owned a great forehand and backhand. And his serve was powerful and accurate.

"[He] certainly is my claim to be the best of all time," said Australian great Rod Laver. "Roger's got all the shots, his anticipation is unbelievable, [and] his . . . backhand is one of the best there is."

Federer was nearly unbeatable at his peak. He won 41 straight matches in 2006 and 2007. From 2003 to 2008, he won 65 consecutive matches on grass courts. And he set an all-time record by being ranked number one in the world for 237 straight weeks.

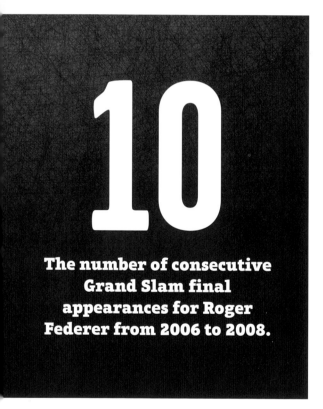

10

The number of consecutive Grand Slam final appearances for Roger Federer from 2006 to 2008.

Roger Federer prepares to rip a backhand at the 2005 US Open.

ROGER FEDERER

Hometown: Basel, Switzerland

Height, Weight: 6 feet 1, 187 pounds

Birth Date: August 8, 1981

Tournament Titles: 80*

Grand Slam Singles Titles: 17*
    Australian Open: 4 (2004, 2006, 2007, 2010)
    French Open: 1 (2009)
    Wimbledon: 7 (2003–07, 2009, 2012)
    US Open: 5 (2004–08)
*Through 2014

SERENA WILLIAMS

Serena Williams had already lost one match point in the 2010 Australian Open finals. There was no way she was going to lose another. She smashed a backhand so hard and so deep that Justine Henin did not even bother swinging at it.

Williams flipped her racket into the air and flopped to her back. It was a sweet victory. It was her fifth championship at the Australian Open. She had also yearned to defeat Henin. The Belgian star had beaten Williams four out of six times in Grand Slam events. But this had been their first meeting in a Grand Slam final, and Williams won when it mattered most.

Few players in history could match the power of a Serena Williams serve.

Williams, a power-hitting American, was used to a more familiar foe. She had beaten sister Venus Williams six times in eight Grand Slam finals, including five straight in 2002 and 2003. It was around then that Serena Williams first rose to number one in the world. She maintained that position for 57 weeks.

At her peak, Williams overpowered most opponents. She controlled points with one of the most powerful serves in women's tennis history. Her forehand was also among the best ever. Her aggressive style resulted in winner after winner from the baseline. She hit enough of them to earn 18 Grand Slam titles through 2014.

Williams is simply one of the most dominant players ever to grace a tennis court.

4

The number of Olympic gold medals Serena Williams won—three in doubles, plus the 2012 singles title in London.

Serena Williams protects the baseline with one of the best forehand shots in the game.

SERENA WILLIAMS

Hometown: Compton, California

Height, Weight: 5 feet 9, 155 pounds

Birth Date: September 26, 1981

Tournament Titles: 63*

Grand Slam Singles Titles: 18*
    Australian Open: 5 (2003, 2005, 2007, 2009, 2010)
    French Open: 2 (2002, 2013)
    Wimbledon: 5 (2002, 2003, 2009, 2010, 2012)
    US Open: 6 (1999, 2002, 2008, 2012–14)
*Through 2014

RAFAEL NADAL

Rafael Nadal's baseline style suited the slow clay courts of the French Open. But critics said he could not overcome the great Roger Federer on the grass at Wimbledon.

Nadal had lost two straight Wimbledon finals to Federer. But in 2008, he had another chance to beat Federer and quiet the critics. Nadal held an 8–7 lead in the fifth set. Three times he had match point. Three times he lost it. But soon an unforced error by Federer gave Nadal his first Wimbledon title.

Nadal fell to his back on the grass in triumph. A month later, he took the number one world ranking away from Federer, who had held it for four years. Nadal won five more Grand Slams in the next two years, including three in 2010 alone.

Rafael Nadal finally overcame Roger Federer to win his first Wimbledon title in 2008.

The muscular Spaniard is among the most aggressive hitters in tennis history. His heavy topspin, speed, and quickness make him a brilliant baseline player. Fellow tennis star Pete Sampras could hardly believe his eyes after watching Nadal play for the first time.

"I'm amazed," he said. "He's able to adjust shots on the run. I have never seen anything like it."

Though Nadal has proven he can win on any surface, he dominates on clay. He won nine French Open titles from 2005 to 2014. No player in tennis history has won more.

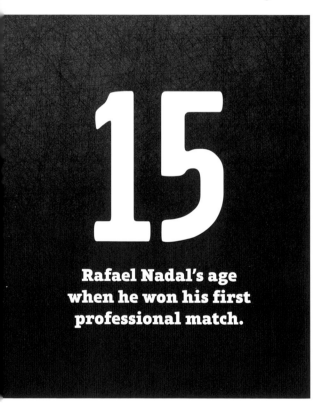

15

Rafael Nadal's age when he won his first professional match.

Rafael Nadal uses his speed and quickness to cover the baseline.

RAFAEL NADAL

Hometown: Manacor, Spain

Height, Weight: 6 feet 1, 187 pounds

Birth Date: June 3, 1986

Tournament Titles: 64*

Grand Slam Singles Titles: 14*
Australian Open: 1 (2009)
French Open: 9 (2005–08, 2010–14)
Wimbledon: 2 (2008, 2010)
US Open: 2 (2010, 2013)

Davis Cup Titles: 4 (2004, 2008, 2009, 2011)
*Through 2014

HONORABLE MENTIONS

Mo Connolly – She won an amazing nine Grand Slam titles in the 1950s before a horseback riding accident ended her career at age 19.

Novak Djokovic – The Serbian beat Rafael Nadal in a 2012 Australian Open final that lasted nearly six hours. It was one of seven Grand Slam titles he won through the 2014 Wimbledon Championships.

Roy Emerson – This 1950s and 1960s Australian superstar ranks fourth on the men's all-time list through 2014 with 12 Grand Slam championships.

Justine Henin – The Belgium native won seven Grand Slam titles, including the French Open four times from 2003 to 2007.

Ivan Lendl – The Czech used his booming serve and powerful baseline game to dominate the sport in the 1980s with 19 Grand Slam finals appearances.

Suzanne Lenglen – A pioneer in French tennis, Lenglen won six Wimbledon titles and two other Grand Slam events from 1919 to 1926.

Fred Perry – The British star won eight of the 16 Grand Slam events played from 1933 to 1936.

Monica Seles – Through 2014, this 1990s standout was the only woman to win three straight Australian and French Open crowns.

Bill Tilden – He won six straight US Championships (1920–25) and seven straight Davis Cups (1920–26), and he became the first American male to win a Wimbledon title (1920).

Helen Wills – Through 2014, this star of the 1920s and 1930s still holds the record for the most Wimbledon titles with eight.

GLOSSARY

baseline
The back line of the tennis court.

ground strokes
Shots players hit after a bounce.

lob
A shot lofted over the head of a player at the net.

match point
A point that can clinch a match victory for a player.

rivalry
A long-standing competition between two players.

stamina
The power to overcome tiring conditions.

tiebreaker
A series of points to decide the winner of a set that reaches a 6-6 tie.

topspin
A shot in which the racket comes off the ball and makes it jump upon landing.

tournament
An event in which players participate to determine a champion.

volley
A shot hit before it bounces, generally close to the net.

FOR MORE INFORMATION

Further Readings

Gitlin, Marty. *Billie Jean King: Tennis Star & Social Activist*. Minneapolis, MN: Abdo Publishing Co., 2011.

Gitlin, Marty. *Tennis*. Minneapolis, MN: Abdo Publishing Co., 2012.

Gitlin, Marty. *Wimbledon*. Minneapolis, MN: Abdo Publishing Co., 2013.

Websites

To learn more about Sports' Best Ever, visit **booklinks.abdopublishing.com**. These links are routinely monitored and updated to provide the most current information available.

INDEX

ABOUT THE AUTHOR

Marty Gitlin is a freelance book writer and sports writer based in Cleveland, Ohio. He has had nearly 100 educational books published since 2006 and also writes for cbssports.com. He earned first place for general excellence as a newspaper sports writer from the Associated Press in 1995. That organization also selected him as one of the top four feature writers in Ohio in 2002.